DOC No. VI.

REPORT

OF THE

SUPERINTENDENT OF PUBLIC INSTRUCTION.

COMMONWEALTH OF VIRGINIA,
OFFICE SUPERINTENDENT PUBLIC INSTRUCTION,
Richmond, March 28th, 1870.

To the General Assembly of Virginia:

GENTLEMEN:

Sensible of the importance of the first duty attached to the office to which I have been elevated by your favor, I should not have ventured to offer my plan of instruction at so early a day, but for the fact that the constitution requires this of the superintendent within thirty days after his election. Having, therefore, no option, and asking indulgence for any imperfections which may be discovered in the work, I beg leave to submit the accompanying "Outline Plan of Public Instruction," which contains the leading features of a permanent system; to which I have appended a "provisional plan for the gradual introduction of the free school system into the state of Virginia." The latter is to be superseded in July, 1871.

I have purposely avoided introducing unsettled questions into the plans. The main features are either such as the constitution requires, or such as have been favorably tested by long experience in other states and countries. Doubtful questions have, as far as possible, been postponed for future consideration. But there are of necessity introduced a few points of detail, which will be seen at once to involve questions of policy, or of constitutional obligation, on which entire unanimity of sentiment cannot be expected, much as it is to be desired. It will be seen, however, that even these few points are practically left unsettled by the provisional plan, which does not ask the legislature to adopt any permanent scheme beyond the plain and imperative requirements of the constitution.

As to the general plan, it will be seen that nothing more is contemplated than the creation of a system of elementary education for children and youth, and of normal schools for the training of teachers; and for the present, nothing more is proposed to be done than the appointing of officers, and the establishing of one to three schools in each county, in order that the people of the state may see the operation of the system. In one sense, the free school system is no longer on trial before us; in another sense, it is on trial. Great doubts and fears regarding it still exist in many honest and intelligent minds, and prejudice has not yet wholly given way. It therefore seems proper, and it may be expected, in undertaking the serious work of introducing this system, that I should give some expression of sentiment in regard to its merits—as I now ask permission to do.

The undeniable fact of the steady growth of the public free school system among the civilized nations, for the last century, creates a presumption in its favor. It flourishes under various forms of government, and, when once tried, is never abandoned, but, on the contrary, is cherished and perfected more and more. It is observed, also, that its popularity is not chiefly among the ignorant and moneyless, but among the more intelligent property holders, and often among those who have the largest taxes to pay. This popularity is not to be accounted for by the growth of the republican form of government; for the system existed on this continent a hundred years before there was a republic; and at this time, it is flourishing among the monarchies of Europe. And would it be seen existing in a perfection unknown on this continent, and vitalizing the energies of a mighty, consolidated empire, behold the kingdom of Prussia! As a mere matter of fact, the public free school system is as clearly established as an element in the world's progress as any other of the great developments of modern enterprise.

We are then forced to the conclusion, that there is something in the system which is regarded by those who have tried it as eminently conducive to the public welfare. What is it? Its philanthropic aspect? No! However benevolent individuals may be, nations are constitutionally selfish. It must contain a source of national aggrandizement, or it would long since have been abandoned.

When the subject is studied as a matter of political economy, it is hard to avoid the conclusion that the nations have persistently maintained their free school systems for the same reason which demands the maintenance of the legislative, executive, and judicial departments of government, namely: that although very costly to maintain, it is more costly to do without; and that the refusal to provide the necessary outlay on the score of economy, would be that sort of "withholding more than is meet, which tendeth to poverty." The idea has certainly taken root among the nations that no money expended in public affairs brings back a larger or surer return of prosperity, than the money expended in the education of the people; and this it does by drying up the great source of crime and pauperism, and by quickening the mind, and thus quickening and guiding the hand of every worker in the land.

Those who have studied the history of pauperism in Southern Europe and in England, tell us that the bulk of it comes from the neglected freedmen of the Roman Empire and of the feudal barons. Now behold the result in the lazzaroni of the Mediterranean states and in the cloud of paupers in England! In the latter, the education of the ruling classes has given national prosperity, but in England every eighth man is a pauper; and whilst she will spend but little for the education of the common people on the free system, she is (or was not long ago) compelled to spend thirty millions a year for the subsistence of her paupers, and a great deal more to punish them for their crimes. The statistics of her prisons show that ninety-five per cent. of crime is committed by persons unable to read or write, and also that not one criminal in two hundred has what may be called an education. And such is the testimony of prisons everywhere as to the intimate relations between ignorance, pauperism, and crime.

When on the other hand, we turn to those European nations which have established public free schools, there is a far better state of things in these particulars. Such is the case in Norway, Sweden, Denmark, Holland, Belgium, and most of the German States. There they have common schools, and there pauperism is almost unknown; and the testimonies go to show that in proportion as the people are educated, they are free from crime and improved in thrift and good morals. Similar results are claimed in those states of our own prosperous and powerful country, where the system has been thoroughly tried, and claimed with the greatest confidence in those states where the system has been longest tried. The outlay is great, but the income is far greater. Nothing is so costly as crime, and ignorant, thriftless labor. Nothing makes public order so difficult, reputation so insecure, property so precarious, government in every department so costly and unstable, as ignorance and vice. Now for these evils, there is within the power of government no remedy so cheap and effectual as common schools, which bring men from darkness into the light. And in these times, when every place and privilege belongs to every man, there is no estimating the stake we have in this matter. Universal suffrage simply necessitates universal education.

The most positive views of the subject are equally forcible, but they cannot here be pursued. I will sum up the whole of what might be said on this subject in one brief, but pregnant, sentence. The world's progress is the outgrowth of educated mind, and in material things, the larger share of it has come from the practical classes. Now a great interest like this, so essential to the prosperity of a state, cannot be safely left to private enterprise, or to the laws of trade. The law of supply and demand has no application in the matter of popular, elementary education, because, in point of fact, the demand for the means of education is in inverse ratio to the supply; in other words, the less the supply the less is the demand: and as for the efficiency of private enterprise in promoting the education of the masses, it is too irregular in its action, too costly in its methods, and too inadequate in its means. Private enterprise never did, and never can educate a whole people. And the public progress demands that the flow of education should be as universal, steady and uninterrupted as the flow of gas and water for the use of a city.

Moreover, the free school system is equally recommended by its comparative cheapness. And this is so from the same causes which render a public system of law more economical than private justice could possibly be, and which render all large and wholesale operations more susceptible of an economical arrangement than smaller. It is quite within bounds to assert that the whole people of Virginia may be educated by the free system for less than one-half of what it now costs to educate less than one-half of her population. In support of this position, I shall hereafter produce the facts and figures.

It should also be remarked that public free schools are not only cheaper than private schools, but as a rule, they are better, and for these reasons, to wit: Every teacher is proved by examination to be competent, the pay is sure and prompt, the schools are organized and conducted by the best methods, the school houses are more comfortable and better provided with school apparatus, and over all is uniform system and intelligent supervision.

The theoretical objections to this system have often been answered, yet as they still start up here and there, it may be well to give them a passing notice. First, it is urged that the free school system is unjust in principle and agrarian in tendency, because people without children have to pay for public education. The answer to that is contained in what has been said before. The system bears exactly the same relation to government that courts and legislatures do, and therefore is a proper object for public support. The saving from losses and prosecutions in the single item of petty larceny, will go far toward paying for the schools. The value added to the laboring population will pay the cost many times over.

As for the principle involved, the state has practically settled that long ago, not only by the well directed support given to her higher institutions, but by contributing to the education of indigent children, and by authoriziug counties to tax themselves for free schools; which many of them have done. She has never before accepted the state system of public free schools, but there have always been many of her first citizens who have been advocates of it. Mr. Jefferson drew out a complete scheme on the state basis, and Governors Campbell and McDowell urged upon the legislature the adoption of the free school system.

Again, it is often urged that free schools tend to weaken parental obligation. I answer this in the words of Professor John B. Minor, who has long been known as a faithful worker in this cause. In an argument on this subject, published more than twenty years ago, he gives the correct answer to this objection by saying: "Free schools do not diminish, much less do they remove, parental responsibility. There is still room for the exercise of the most anxious care—with the additional motive to it that whatever care is bestowed will result in good, not to the children of one family only, but to those of an entire community. * * * Free schools do not diminish responsibility; on the contrary, they awaken it; they stimulate it to an ardent, glowing zeal; and they supply the means to make it achieve the most valuable results."

A graver objection than all others is urged, when it is affirmed that the free school system inclines the people to religious error and impiety. This is answered by a simple and emphatic denial. It would be strange, indeed, if well-ordered schools, located in the bosom of christian neighborhoods, should lead to such results. Is ignorance the mother of devotion, after all that has been said to the contrary? Far from it! Knowledge is the guide to truth and piety; ignorance the mother of error and sin. Moreover, the moral influence pervading every school will be just the influence pervading the neighborhood in which it is carried on. Every properly conducted school itself, furnishes an admirable moral as well as intellectual discipline. Immoral teachers may often be found in private schools, but in public schools—never! And it is an established fact, that the vast majority of teachers in public schools are personally religious, and most active in promoting Sunday schools, and in doing good generally. Truth and piety have everything to hope for—nothing to fear—from public free schools. I express myself with the more confidence on this point because it has been one of anxiety with myself, and the opposite view has been driven out of my mind by a careful study of the subject.

An objection is sometimes based on the sparseness of our population; but this fact really furnishes a strong argument in its favor. Where the population is so thin as not to be able to furnish a minimum number of pupils within reach of a school-house, then there can be no school allowed there, and if the private school system can supply the desideratum it will have a clear field for doing so. But where a school is practicable at all, it can be furnished far more cheaply, regularly and certainly, by the public than by the private system.

Allow me, gentlemen, to add two additional remarks, and I will conclude these hastily expressed, though not hastily adopted, views on this important subject.

Virginia, for the first time as a state, is entering upon the systematic production of the most valuable commodity which can be possessed by a state or offered in the markets of the world—namely, *trained mind!* Nothing else commands so high a price, or produces such large results. Men are valued everywhere, not in proportion to their brute force, or even their natural endowments, but in proportion to their knowledge, skill, and habits of industry. Slumbering intellect and untrained fingers can command but little more wages than the powers of the brute. In every grade of employment intelligence adds to the value of the labor, and in the same proportion to the wealth of the state. There is no question connected with this subject that is more interesting, and none that will bear a closer examination, than the commercial value of popular education. When mind utters its workings in the form of reapers, manures, cotton gins, printing presses, railroads and steamboats, one can easily see that the cost of educating a generation is paid by the production of a few men like Watt and Whitney, Edmund Ruffin and Cyrus McCormack. But it is not so obvious, yet equally true, that popular education constantly produces an infinite variety of similar results, which, when taken singly, may attract but limited notice, yet occurring, as they do, in every department of effort, their combined influence on the prosperity of the state is prodigious. And this influence is not confined to the production of new inventions, but is everywhere stimulating and improving the quality of labor, so that the aggregate of the unnoticed results far more than returns all its cost to the state.

One other vital consideration presses this matter upon our attention at this critical time. Immigration will avoid a state which has not a good free school system in operation. Mechanics and farmers, in choosing a home, will always be largely influenced by the educational facilities of a country. Mechanics know that they had better take low wages, farmers know that they had better pay higher prices for land, where there are public schools, than where they would have to depend on the costly, troublesome and uncertain mode of hunting up means of education by private effort. This consideration will influence also the rich capitalists just as much as men of smaller means. If capitalists buy lands, establish factories, open mines, or build railroads, their success is dependent upon attracting laborers, small producers and large patronage. Almost every other state in the Union is ahead of us in this matter.

In conclusion, I beg leave to call attention to the fact that my strong convictions as to the value of the free school system has not caused me to forget the straitened condition of our suffering state. I therefore propose, as will be seen by reference to my provisional plan, that we should commence on the smallest scale at all compatible with our constitutional obligations.

I am, very respectfully,

Your obedient servant,

W. H. RUFFNER,

Superintendent of Public Instruction.

OUTLINE PLAN OF PUBLIC INSTRUCTION FOR THE STATE OF VIRGINIA.

ARTICLE I.

Officers.

SECTION 1. 1. Board of Education.
2. State Superintendent of Public Instruction.
3. County Superintendents.
4. District Trustees.

ARTICLE II.

The Board of Education.

SEC. 2. Shall consist of the governor, the state superintendent, and the attorney-general.

SEC. 3. Their duties shall be—

1. To suggest improvements in the laws.
2. To appoint and remove county superintendents, subject to the action of the senate.
3. To manage school funds.
4. To provide for uniformity of text-books, and for supplying indigent children with text-books free of charge, and school-houses with apparatus; all as hereafter prescribed by law.
5. To decide appeals from decisions of the state superintendent.
6. To prescribe and order payment for whatever is necessary for the superintendent's office; also to order payment of his necessary traveling expenses; not to exceed ——— dollars for office expenditures, and ——— for traveling expenses.
7. Tó audit all accounts claiming payment from the school funds.
8. To do all that is necessary to secure the carrying out of the school laws.
9. To hire such clerical service as may be necessary for the office; not exceeding——— dollars.
10. To report annually to the legislature.

ARTICLE III.

State Superintendent of Public Instruction.

SEC. 4. He shall be elected as prescribed by the constitution, and his salary fixed by law.

SEC. 5. He shall be required to have an office at the capital; which office shall be provided by the state.

SEC. 6. His duties shall be—

1. To enforce the school laws and regulations.
2. To advise and instruct county superintendents and to supervise free schools.

3. To apportion school moneys according to the ratio prescribed by the constitution, and to furnish an abstract of such apportionment to the state auditor and to the county superintendent and county treasurer of each county, keeping the same on file in his own office.

4. To prepare and supply to the local officers and teachers suitable printed forms and copies of school laws and regulations.

5. To decide appeals.

6. To preserve a record of his own decisions.

7. To preserve in his office school documents, school books, apparatus, maps, charts, et cet., provided they are obtained without cost to the state.

8. To provide a seal for his office.

9. To require reports from county superintendents.

10. To make suggestions and an annual report to the board of education.

ARTICLE IV.

County superintendents.

Sec. 7. The county superintendents chosen as above stated, shall continue in office during good behavior, not longer than three years, unless re-elected.

Sec. 8. Their remuneration should be such as to secure competent men for the position, and enable them to give all needed time to the work required. In form, the pay should be partly fixed, and partly contingent on results accomplished.

Sec. 9. The duties of each county superintendent shall be—

1. To explain the school system.

2. To provide for submitting to popular vote the question of county appropriations.

3. To apportion school money under instruction by the board of education, and to furnish copies of his apportionment to the state superintendent, to the county treasurer, and to the clerk of each district board of trustees.

4. To withhold appropriations from such districts as fail to comply with regulations.

5. To appoint trustees to fill vacancies.

6. To examine teachers and grant certificates.

7. To promote the improvement of teachers.

8. To attend the organization of district boards, and always to be a corresponding member thereof.

9. To visit schools.

10. To hear appeals.

11. To require reports from district clerks and teachers.

12. To report to the state superintendent, and to be subject to his control and direction.

ARTICLE V.

District trustees.

Sec. 10. The number and term of office shall be as specified in the constitution.

Sec. 11. Trustees may be elected or appointed. (In some states they are appointed by the board of education; in others, elected by the people. It is highly desirable that at least the first trustees should be appointed by the board of education.)

Sec. 12. Every school trustee and teacher shall be exempt from serving on juries, from working on roads (but not from any road tax), and from militia duty in time of peace.

Sec. 13. Each board of trustees shall hold their first meeting at the call of the county superintendent, and at this meeting they shall choose one of their number clerk of the board, and also make provision for taking the census of children in the district and collecting educational statistics.

Sec. 14. The clerk shall keep a record of the proceedings, and be the agent of the board; for which, suitable compensation shall be allowed him out of the funds of the district.

Sec. 15. The duties of the board of trustees shall be—

1. To make and enforce rules.
2. To employ and dismiss teachers, under restrictions.
3. To dismiss pupils.
4. To take census of children.
5. To call meetings of voters.
6. To provide and manage school property.
7. To report annually to the county superintendents.

ARTICLE VI.

Districts.

Sec. 16. Districts shall be named or numbered by the county superintendent.

Sec. 17. Until further provided, the districts shall be coterminous with the townships.

Sec. 18. Each district shall be a body corporate.

ARTICLE VII.

General rules for officers.

Sec. 19. Every teacher and officer shall have the right of appeal, under regulations.

Sec. 20. No teacher or officer shall be interested pecuniarily in the sale of school books or other school material.

Sec. 21. Higher authorities may discharge the neglected duties of lower, under restrictions.

ARTICLE VIII.

Teachers.

Sec. 22. 1. Must hold certificates.
2. Must keep a register and make reports.
3. May suspend pupils until the board acts.

ARTICLE IX.

Schools.

Sec. 23. The expense of schools shall be borne by the state, county, and district, in such proportion as shall be determined hereafter. In general, one-half the cost of instruction shall be paid from the state money and the other half from the county money; the other school expenses by the district.

Sec. 24. Not less than five months of time, and a certain average attendance required, in order to receive the state money.

Sec. 25. The schools shall be free to all persons belonging to the district between the ages of five and twenty-one years, and, in special cases, to those belonging to other districts, under certain uniform regulations.

Sec. 26. Separate schools shall be provided for white and colored children, under the same general regulations.

Sec. 27. Special and equitable provision shall be made whereby minorities in a district, who might under the general law be deprived of the benefits of education, may enjoy a proportionate share of the school funds.

Sec. 28. Trustees may receive special donations in support of schools.

Sec. 29. The studies in every school shall be orthography, reading, writing, arithmetic, grammar, geography; others allowed only under restrictions.

Sec. 30. Graded schools shall be allowed under suitable regulations: provided, always, that the branches named above shall constitute the body of the course.

Sec. 31. Normal schools shall be established as soon as practicable.

ARTICLE X.

School Funds.

Sec. 32. The sources of revenue shall be those set apart and ordered by the constitution.

Sec. 33. The state school funds shall be kept by the state treasurer in separate accounts, and shall never be used for any other purpose than the maintenance of the public free school system.

Sec. 34. The salaries of the county superintendents, so far as payable by the state, shall be paid out of the bulk of the school funds, as distinguished from the apportionments to counties.

Sec. 35. At the proper time each county treasurer shall make requisition in due form for the total amount of money coming to the county from the state treasurer, which, when approved by the state superintendent, shall be paid in the usual way.

Sec. 36. All school moneys to be disbursed in each county shall be in the custody of the county treasurer thereof, for which provision shall be made in his bond. Separate accounts shall be kept of the state, county, and district funds, and they shall be paid out on orders of the district clerk, approved by the county superintendent; each order to state on its face the object to which the money is to be applied: provided, that the county superintendent shall draw through the state superintendent for his own pay.

Sec. 37. County and district taxes shall be assessed and collected like other taxes.

Sec. 38. Unexpended portions of state money in the several counties shall be held subject to redivision the next year.

ARTICLE XI.

City Organizations.

SEC. 39. Public free school systems now in successful operation in cities shall be allowed to continue without change until farther legislation: provided, that such cities shall not be exempted from the state tax, and may receive their share of school money.

PROVISIONAL PLAN

FOR THE GRADUAL INTRODUCTION OF THE PUBLIC FREE SCHOOL SYSTEM INTO THE STATE OF VIRGINIA.

---

1. The outline plan preceding this shall be adopted provisionally, except so far as it is modified by this plan.

2. The capitation tax increased to one dollar shall be immediately set apart for the introduction of the free school system, and be collected with the taxes for this year.

3. The board of education shall proceed with due diligence and caution, by the help of the agency hereinafter provided, to appoint county superintendents for the whole state, and also to appoint all the district trustees required by the constitution.

4. The salaries of county superintendents shall be fixed hereafter; but until otherwise provided, these officers may be paid not exceeding three dollars a day, for every day of actual service rendered.

5. All appointments of county superintendents made during the session of the general assembly, shall be subject to the immediate action of the senate; but such superintendents as may be appointed after the adjournment of the present legislature, and before the assembling of the next, shall be allowed to discharge the duties and receive the pay attached to the office, until an opportunity occurs for the action of the senate.

6. In order to assist in the difficult work of introducing the system, the board of education shall be authorized to appoint an agent temporarily in each congressional district. The duties of this agent shall be to aid the board of education in selecting officers for the counties and districts, and to co-operate with those officers in explaining the free school system to the people, and in providing for the establishment of the first schools. The board shall be authorized to pay this agent, or circuit superintendent, not exceeding six dollars ($6) a day, for every day of actual service rendered, and to allow that his travelling expenses may be paid by the counties in which he operates: provided, that not more than twenty-five thousand dollars ($25,000) of the state money shall be expended in paying county and circuit superintendents up to July 1, 1871.

7. The board of education shall be required to attach counties which, by the census of 1860, contained less than 8,000 inhabitants, to adjoining counties, in assigning territory to county superintendents.

8. In making up the school estimate to be submitted to county vote, there shall be included an allowance for the incidental expenses of county and circuit superintendents; the maximum amount to be named by the board of education.

9. At the proper time the board of education shall apportion the state money among the counties according to population: provided, that no county shall be neglected, and that a fair proportion be observed between white and colored schools; and provided that the general basis on which the schools are established shall be an equal division of the cost of instruction between the state and counties, with school-house expenses borne by districts. This does not apply to cities now having free schools supported by taxation.

10. The location of the first school or schools in a county shall be determined by a convention of the district trustees, called and presided over by the county superintendent, after the vote has been taken and given in favor of the county appropriation; all under general instructions by the board of education.

11. Each city or town of more than 5,000 inhabitants, not having in successful operation a free school system, shall be a school district.

12. This plan shall continue in force until July 1, 1871.

www.ingramcontent.com/pod-product-compliance
Lightning Source LLC
LaVergne TN
LVHW020643110826
845149LV00004B/1325

* 9 7 8 1 4 1 8 1 8 9 4 6 4 *